THE BACK AND THE FRONT OF IT

THE BACK
and the
FRONT
of it

Connie Bensley

BLOODAXE BOOKS

ISBN: 1 85224 518 2

First published 2000 by
Bloodaxe Books Ltd,
P.O. Box 1SN,
Newcastle upon Tyne NE99 1SN.

Bloodaxe Books Ltd acknowledges
the financial assistance of Northern Arts.

northern
arts

Cover printing by J. Thomson Colour Printers Ltd, Glasgow.

Printed in Great Britain by
Cromwell Press Ltd, Trowbridge, Wiltshire.

for
Felicity Napier
Jill Hepple
Kris Nielsen Fehn
John Pattenden

Acknowledgements

Acknowledgements are due to the editors of the following publications where some of these poems first appeared: *Agenda, The Express, The Independent, The North, Orbis, Poetry Review, The Rialto, Seam, The Spectator, Sunk Island Review* and *The Times Literary Supplement.*

Contents

Apologia

My life is too dull and too careful –
even I can see that:
the orderly bedside table,
the spoilt cat.

Surely I should have been bolder.
What could biographers say?
*She got up, ate toast and went shopping
day after day?*

Whisky and gin are alarming,
Ecstasy makes you drop dead.
Toy boys make inroads on cash
and your half of the bed.

Emily Dickinson, help me.
Stevie, look up from your Aunt.
Some people can stand excitement,
some people can't.

The Back and the Front of It

While she marvels at the brilliance
of the peacock, he walks off to study
its back, the dun-coloured feathers,
the muscular plaque which raises the fabulous fan,
the picking-through-broken-glass gait.

While she relishes linen and silver,
leather-bound menus, rosy light
gleaming on brilliantined waiters
he tries to catch a glimpse
of the steamy, sweating kitchens.

And while she is smitten by the tightrope walkers,
their sequins flashing perilously from side to side;
the peachy acrobats with their hoops of fire
and the haughty Balinski Brothers, golden limbed
in their human pyramid –

he escapes to the rear of the tent
and joins the jugglers as they knock back
bottles of stout, pick at loose bits
of shine and glitter, belch, yawn,
rub their ankles, pick their teeth.

These two are always out of step.
Surely it can't last, but which
will be the first to stray? This is the question
which brings the clowns running,
with their jibes, their pointing fingers.

Taking a Taxi to a Wedding

My driver is on his second marriage:
'It's a gamble isn't it?' he says.
The first one was a long disappointment
but now he's happy – delirious almost.
They holiday in France: red wine
and camping come into the story
repeatedly. The new wife loves both.
She also makes tea for his cricket team.
I imagine her blonde hair swinging
over the bread and butter, her short skirt
riding up over tanned thighs. But
'She's older than me,' he adds,
slipping, eel-like, through an amber light,
'and she's mad about me.' He elaborates;
touches in frank details of their love...
All this between Putney and Ladbroke Grove.

Rewards

To those who have
shall be given:

the prize to the winners
lovers to the beautiful,

tributes to the rich,
empires to the bold.

Settle the meek
into their corners

for an interminable wait.

In Passing

I gave him everything:
rush lights, a pillow of herbs,
dreams like seed packets
and massage with scented oils.

He gave me a red-beaked bird,
a stone with a golden vein,
his poste restante address: and a child
so that I could bear him in mind.

The Go-Between

My fiancé, bitchy to the last,
gave me as a parting gift a parrot
whose only tongue was Greek. But by the way
it spoke, I felt quite sure the bird
insulted me. His spiteful eye shot messages
of hate, and at the end of every speech
he climaxed on a fusillade of shrieks.

I bought a textbook on demotic Greek;
I joined a class; struck up a loose rapport
with waiters in a local Greek café
(a grave mistake – but that's another tale)
still nobody could give a clear account
of what the bird's discourse could mean.
                                        At length
I taught him certain Anglo-Saxon words
and sent him back by cab. He disappeared
shouting the worst obscenities I knew,
turning the air a rich and vibrant blue.

Sanatorium
Norfolk 1955

A dozen people have driven up to see me
this summer – Ratty, the Zieglers, Pixie and so on.
They tour the Norfolk churches, then come on here.
We have tea in my room: they bring cake
and I set myself to be anecdotal.
We have a convivial time, but I finally wilt
under the pressure to be entertaining.
Patients must be entertaining, or who will visit them?

And it's difficult to find space for them, my room
is so untidy. Even the bedside table is deplorable:
yesterday's ashtray unemptied, yesterday's *Times* unread,
the foul-tasting agar-agar which I don't now need
thanks to the laxative effect of P.A.S.,
the mirror for shaving, the extra socks (no heating
until October), my blue silk spotted scarf,
two boxes of Marcovitch, a file marked 'TO DO, May 12'.

Charlie, the male nurse, has just turned up
to take last night's bottle, followed by Mrs May
for the hoovering. She skirts the thunderbox
and tells me she's going to see her daughter
in America next month on the Queen Mary (£120 return,
she's saved up). I'm on my best behaviour with Mrs M.
because she once told me I looked like
Rex Harrison. I felt much better that day.

Some people send me improving books (perhaps they think
there's time for a quick conversion) – books about
Billy Graham and Ouspensky, books on Christianity
and Being Saved. This seems ominous, and rather a cheek.
But I do find that thinking, even for short spells,
is interesting. I've taken to doing it in the morning
when they bring the tea, but not for more than
ten minutes, with no mind-wandering allowed.

This week I'm thinking about Buddhism,
one of the eight-fold paths each day.
I look forward to seeing the effect
after a month. One thing I've already noticed
is that other people's actions are often
frightfully wrong. I ponder this over breakfast –
brassy tea, toast like linoleum, a dispirited egg,
two sachets of P.A.S. which I force down;

and now here comes the shopper – a German girl,
married to the thoracoplasty in room 49. I order
chocolate and writing paper, and she takes £1
from my wallet. This is kept in the fruit bowl,
on top of the spare bulb which I inherited from
my friend, de Musset, who had room 8. He used it
to keep his terrapins warm. What became of them, after
he died? We've stopped asking questions like that.

Politesse

Across the table he watches his ex-wife.
She is laughing and murmuring with her new husband.

It reminds him of his train journey
earlier that day, when a crowd of tourists
surged into his carriage. One of them
made some sort of speech, impenetrable
and guttural; the rest responded
with wild laughter, slapping their knees,
beaming into each others' faces.

He felt obliged to smile, though the smile itself
was stiff and dry as papier-mâché.

'The Unexamined Life is not Worth Living'

Taking the hint from Socrates,
he examined his life daily –
that unwieldy, shape-shifting thing.
Under a microscope, bits of it
looked promising, bits of it moribund.

His preoccupations remained constant:
first, how to become magnetic and rich
without getting out of bed too early
in the morning; next, how to stay calm
in the face of incipient baldness.

Natural Selection

Get rid of that Dog
he frowned – but died himself. She
and Dog exchanged smiles.

Cut

I don't like the company you're keeping:
fringe musicians, boom operators,
best boys. Why can't you be like your father
and polish up a decent game of golf?
That's where he found me, you know,
at the nineteenth hole.

Things to do?
But you've only just come.

Twelve Things I Don't Want to Hear

Assemble this in eight straightforward steps.
Start with a fish stock, made the day before.
The driver has arrived but, sadly, drunk.
We'll need some disinfectant for the floor.

Ensure all surfaces are clean and dry.
There's been a problem, Madam, I'm afraid!
We'd better have the manhole cover up.
Apologies, the doctor's been delayed.

I'd love to bring a friend, he's so depressed.
They've put you on the camp bed in the hall.
There's just one table left, perhaps you'd share?
I know it's midnight, but I had to call...

Emperor

I rise at six, clean my teeth
with paste and then powdered coral,

scrape my tongue, and rinse my mouth
with brandy and water.

An hour is spent in the bath,
while my papers are read aloud to me.

I shave with a razor from Britain;
Eau de Cologne is brushed into my chest

and then I am dressed. My boots are broken in
by my valet, who must always be chosen

with this in mind. I take my snuff box
and my handkerchief, and am at my desk by nine.

My troops wait in their bivouacs. Maps unfurl
their contours, and all Europe is under my hand.

Lodger

We've got Rasputin in the potting shed now.
He has a real gift for cuttings and propagation.
You'd think the cold would kill him off
but he's tough: you only have to look at the scars
when he's standing at the kitchen sink
having a wash.

Language isn't much of a problem: his gestures are
eloquent. He has an affinity with wild things.
When Coco had enteritis he uttered special
incantations and made infusions of wild herbs
to rub into her fur.

No, she didn't recover.

Birth Day

The ear will know first – that complexity
of cochlea, stirrup, drum.

But the phone is silent.

Somewhere, on rucked sheets,
you are pushing, thrashing, groaning
in a rush of sweat and blood.

Here, we gaze absently from the window

at the ice-cream-white buds of the magnolia
splitting out of their brown jackets. Time stops.

It has given up trying to match the clock.

Grit in the Oyster

I don't know why I wear this watch:
it has a creative attitude to time –
sometimes it agrees with Greenwich,
sometimes it has quixotic ideas of its own –
lagging lazily or racing playfully ahead.

It has such a clear, lucid face.
The strap, also, conveys conviction.
But it is often quite mad at night,
proposing ludicrous theories at dawn.
And how does it know it is night?

It can be finicky and precise
for days on end, lulling me
into gullibility. Then it runs amok
ruining my rendezvous and bringing me
late and panicky to station platforms.

Why not wrap it in a cloth and smash it
with a mallet, as conjurors do?
                              We who lead
quiet lives need a spice of unreliability,
like the steady woman marrying a crook
or the staid professor falling for a Lolita.

Get a Life

When the child was born
there were long faces and tears
but after a while, despair was folded away
and planning began.

The baby's feet
flexed and grasped, practised
their stand-in role.
The baby smiled on cue, generously.

Later, she rolled, bounced,
sang, drew a house with her feet
and put herself in the garden.
She gave herself arms

and ordinary hands. Stopped.
Rubbed them out
using her special long rubber
and sat silent till tea time.

Onward and upward: a stony path,
a sunny nature, a profession.
People bring their troubles to her desk.
Her light burns on into the night.

Insomnia

It's like waiting for someone to leave –
someone tedious, garrulous
and worryingly manic.
Someone full of reminiscences
which you don't want to hear about.

It's like waiting for something
to be taken away – something
with a buzz as maddening as tinnitus;
something you've grown tired of, which is
taking up space.

These things multiply, creak and throw shadows
round the room. They start asking
upsetting questions.
Lie doggo. This is not
an interrogation chamber.

The clock strikes again.
To pass the time,
you could try making up anagrams.
You could start with
ABSENCE and OBLIVION.

Time Traveller

Talking to a man in a pub,
Jesus recaps: 'The body
opened up, you say?
The heart of the man cut out
and a pig's heart sewn in,
beating like an eagle's wing?

And on the Third Day, the man
rises up and walks!
Who performs this miracle,
and what words does he say
to make it come to pass?'

Bonus

In the first warm sun of the year,
to raise my spirits from zero,
I get in my car and drive to the garden centre
and there, pushing a trolley
like an ordinary person,
is a Famous Actor.

Is it? Yes it is. I hear his voice,
low but unmistakable,
asking about potting compost.
His chestnut hair, his leather jacket
gleam. He doesn't look
at the price of anything.

I choose Heartsease, while he muses
over something more flamboyant.
The darkness of his glasses! The brightness
of his signet ring! I turn away,
but by chance we pass and repass
along the leafy arbours

Blossom rains down on us
festive as a wedding.
At the checkout, our trolleys touch
but I do not speak, except to murmur *sorry*
when his Garrya Elliptica
falls on top of my Maidenhair Fern.

Reflection

An old neck in a gold chain
an old foot in a silver shoe:

an old fool in a new dress –
I wouldn't be her, would you?

A new love in an old bed?
She'll find more than the springs will creak:

she'd far better the armchair.
(Remind her again next week.)

English Dictation

I

I woke up from my nap. The clock struck four.
I thought I'd go out on a City Tour.
I rang Reception. *Tours leave on the hour.*
I booked one: but the rain began to pour.

Still, better go. It made me think of our
debacle when we spent the day in Tours.
The trees were caked with ice and white as flour,
we got lost in the snow and found that dour

café – where waiters (and the wine) were sour.
The former looked askance at our amour –
quite right. It ended. Now I just devour
my guide books on another lonely tour.

II

The tour raised up my spirits from their trough.
We drank some wine. I met a man from Slough
who got us singing on the coach – although
I got fed up with 'Blossom on the Bough'.

But when I staggered back I felt quite rough.
I rang Reception, said: *I've got a cough.*
I need some pills and whiskey. She said: *Tough.*
I saw you coming in. You've had enough.

The Visit

They were acting out a tiresome folie à deux:
quarrelling as they arrived on the doorstep;
laughing and bickering over the drinks,
and then enacting some drama involving
mobile phones and third parties. We put up with it,
heavy with our married politeness and wry smiles,
though the charged air skewed the evening.
After they left (shouted farewells in the street,
the car revving up a storm) peace floated down
like feathers. But we felt dull. In bed
we recalled the days of our own capriciousness
and lay frowning, not at all at rest.

Holding Hands in the Movie Show

That first time: I was sixteen
and so was he. Difficult to know
who was more nervous. His hand
creeping over the armrest,
infinitesimally slow,
his shoulder touching mine, my heart
in a frenzy, the film a vague blur.

It was that sort of era –
or I was that sort of innocent.
But once the virginity of my palm was breached –
what delicious, eloquent hand-holdings:
passionate squeezes, delicate tracings
and strokings – furtive and illicit, perhaps,
or familiar, comforting.

Cut to half a century later,
to a grandchild, frightened
by a monster on the giant screen.
A head burrows into my shoulder,
a hand clutches mine, hanging on for dear life.
'Come on, be brave,' I murmur,
'it'll all be over soon.'

Metropolitan

The city's manic, but my Love is sane.
He likes the hustle – doesn't want to move.
My Love's not only urban, but urbane.

I'd leave tomorrow – gladly pack it in,
but he prefers the lamplight to the stars.
We lie in bed marooned inside the din.

He has to stay in reach of Waterloo.
He has to travel in the outside lane.
I tell him that I've grown to like it too.
That's love. You stack the loss against the gain.

Levelling

Where the big house burned down
is now a geometry of tennis courts,
hard and municipal in the vertical light.
But where is the lake?

It is curtained by the sweep of trees,
sudden and mysterious as before.
The Japanese bridge has gone
and the black rowing boat

but still there are lilies
nudged by burly, snapping carp;
and any day now, creepers will blindfold
the notice which threatens trespassers.

This is the remnant
of that leafy, rambling seclusion –
follies and balustrades,
the frivolous summerhouse.

It must have been hard
to strip and level so much ground.
The playing fields stretch out
flat as biscuits, to the horizon.

Leviathan

Something has grown too big for the pond:
first the moorhens disappeared
then the ducks (corner-of-the-eye stuff,
nothing strictly attributable).
The Canada Geese stayed, but looked as if they knew
something they'd rather not think about.

A goat on the village green went mad overnight.
Then pensioners living nearby
started to peg out: heart attacks mostly
and always at Meals-on-Wheels time
(the body on the rug, the cartons emptied).
Alice Weevil went missing altogether.

A builder up a ladder, on his mobile,
didn't at first hear the flub of something
working its way up the rungs behind him.
'Quick Reg,' were his last words –
'get the pond drained – don't wait
for the Council – there's a huge, unbelievable –'

The R Word

I meant us to have a good life together:
trading words and gestures, achieving
some sort of closeness.
But it isn't working out like that.

Fragments of fruit fall, spurned
to the bottom of your cage
while you crouch, moping, in the corner.

Come on, it's not as if you ever lived
in a tree. The jungle
would be worse for you than SW13.

But the sky through the kitchen window seems
alien, and you flinch at the great predators,
roaring nose-to-tail on the flight path.

I flinch too. I realise I've taken on
what I always try to shirk.

Responsibility.

Escape

Of course she has to shout at him sometimes.
He hides his hearing aid in strange places:
in the fridge, in the teapot, under the carpet.

He follows her round, yet is no longer there
though some relic remains – intractable,
regressed, uttering an eternal chorus:
Where are you going? Where going?
Where? Where going?

They face each other across the hearth
in the evenings. One night
she slides low in her chair,
the evening paper swooping whitely
to the floor. At dawn he is still talking:
Where? Where are you going? Where going?

Ice Cream

It can't be the cornet I've just bought
from NICO'S ICE CREAM PARLOUR

and it isn't the unseasonable weather –
warm sun confounding the Christmas shoppers.

What is it? I rest my carrier bags
on a low wall outside Laura Ashley

and gaze at the market – customers hefting
melons; pigeons lined up on the roof of GAP,

stalls shining with aubergines, oranges, peppers,
vans unloading in organised chaos.

I take another mouthful of sweetness;
and euphoria turns to ecstasy, real and sharp.

You might not think it much of an epiphany.
You might think it's just a hormonal quirk.

I reach the bottom of the cornet
and even the last mouthful is succulent.

At Kill-Two-Birds

I am raising an army of mercenaries.
Any pensioner may apply – preference given
to the suicidal, the cranky, and those
who believe in sending a gunboat.

Much of the fighting will be technical
and sedentary; but a full sacrifice of casualties
is also planned. Medals will be freely awarded.
Enlist today. Bus with ramp collects.

Getting Out of Hand

Experimenting with virtual reality
she calls up a good-sized house, and in it she pops
Rupert Brooke, who comes out of his study
muttering octosyllabics and twisting
his inky fingers through his famous hair.

Remembering his penchant for anguished passion
she summons Charlotte Brontë – but something goes wrong
and it is Branwell who turns up, though it doesn't seem
to matter, and he falls into conversation with Rupert
about the rail service to Lulworth Cove.

They settle down for tea, and here comes Jane Austen
handing round the bread and butter. Cup in hand,
she leafs through a volume of diaries
found on the coffee table. Her eyes widen
and she drops the book with a nervous glance

over her shoulder, but there is no sign
of the author, for Joe Orton (if on the premises)
is engaged elsewhere. More figures
materialise, and surely someone will have to wash
the cups – though that doesn't look like a butler

limping in through the French windows, saturnine
and patrician, with a dangerous-looking hound in tow.
Someone who understands these animals is needed a.s.a.p.
and Conan Doyle springs to mind – being also qualified
to advise about the foot – but no, surely that's GBS

cycling bossily up through the garden
ready to sort everyone out, if he can make himself heard
above the shouting and barking. Now they're all
comparing something, and fragments of speech surface:
Missolonghi... mosquito... my best apple tree.

In the Palm of His Hand

I'm in love, I'm in love!
I know – I've cried Wolf before
but this time it's true.
I'm in for the full agony:
the contrived encounters;
the heart-shock of the doorbell;
the new meaning to life; the new lingerie.

How do I know it will get that far?
Because of his meaningful look
when he weighs my mange-tout, my pink fir apples.
Because he slips an extra nectarine into my basket.
Because on Tuesday he offered to deliver
to me personally, and he wrote my address
in the palm of his hand.

Faint Hopes

Driving him to the station for the last train,
she resolved that next time she would be
more entertaining, sexier, choose a better wine.

On the platform he didn't even offer
his usual playful insults – merely eyed
the dull graffiti, stifling a yawn.

The silence was awkward. Outside
a car set up a wail, clamouring for relief
in a glissando of outrage and distress.

What Went Wrong?

He did his best to love her, it is true,
although his hopes were tenuous and slender.
He summoned up politeness, kindness too.
But lust? Bad luck. She wasn't the right gender.

House Detective

My heartbeat imitates a castanet.
The sofa wears its dustsheet like a pall.
The house is manifestly empty. Yet
the floorboards creak across the empty hall.

The telephone is ringing by the bed.
The door's alarmed; the desk is quite distressed.
The empty car is singing by the kerb.
I think you've gone. I think it's for the best.

Impediment

Dreaming that I'd agreed to marry your son
was embarrassing: his boyish letter
made it worse. *It will be great –*
every night you can help me with my calculus.

A recantation was frantically needed
but all my pens turned blank in my hand.
Some nightmares are worse
than the creak of an axeman on the stair.

Home Truths

The three of us were having tea, I remember,
second cups and walnut cake going round
when my sister started singing the praises of Dorchester
and right away, taking another slice,
Dave went into raptures about the place –
Dorchester this, Dorchester that.
I said: *What are you talking about Dave?*
I'm sure we've never been there.
He just stirred his tea with a knowing smile.
I was put out, miffed. What call
had he got to gang up with my sister like that?
Some betrayals are so small
you can hardly put your finger on them
at the time.

Time to Part

He thought if he could see her just once more
and hold her hand and – most important – touch
her heart, they'd be all right. They met for lunch.
He noticed she kept looking at her watch.

He ordered oysters, veal, a decent wine.
He said how very cold it was for March.
He couldn't taste the food. He took her hand
to stop her looking slyly at her watch.

She waved aside the gâteaux. In despair
he tried to keep her, offered her a peach.
The restaurant was silent as a church.
The waiter, leaning idly, tapped his watch.

She gathered her belongings with a smile.
but he fell silent. Too late now for speech.
Her platitudes delayed them at the door.
He watched her go. He watched her out of reach.

Absconded

Mrs Moncrieff, J.P.,
climbed down from the bench one day
and held out her hand
to a young delinquent
with tense muscles, a ponytail
and a butterfly tattoo.

No one has seen them since.

The Melon Seller

This man has been standing by his melons
for hours. He hefts one like a hand grenade,
looks mournful. Something is wrong with his salesmanship.

Round him, crowds swirl up from the underground.
They look through him, as he lolls
by his stall, his throat worn out by bawling.

Short skirts, brown legs brush past him.
He wants to be squeezed, nuzzled, nibbled
by mellifluous lemon-scented lovers.

He scowls at his golden spoiling fruits, longs
to drown them, imagines their fair little heads bobbing
down to the sea, leaving him unburdened, footloose, free.

The Yellow Scarf

You left your yellow scarf beside the pool.
I wind it round my wrist in bed at night.
Will you come back? Nobody but a fool
would take you back. And yes, of course, you're right,
I would.
       Each day I walk down to the quay,
under the sky's inert and mocking blue.
I haunt the beach and listen to the sea
trying to make its mind up what to do.

And now, while shaving, seeing myself plain –
the tic, the hollow cheek, the anxious stare –
I know I have to follow you. The pain
won't otherwise be eased, that much is clear.
I pack my bag, feeling a surge of hope.
I put your scarf in last, twisted into a rope.

The Aspirant

Don't look any further. If you want a victim,
take me. No matter how blunt the knife
or the words, choose me.

A spanner, an icicle, a scythe,
it's all the same: on a towpath
or in a bed at night.

I hang around auditions.
Most are trying for the murderer
but I covet the other role.

But it will go to someone else.
Someone wrong, but within reach,
A good girl, pillar of the local church.

Psychopaths with shards of glass,
let me pass without a glance.
Wallflower. I'm not invited for this dance.

That Old Black Magic

I was working in the animal jail
at the time: swabbing out the parrots,
hosing down the chihuahuas,
fingerprinting the baboons,
when the revelation struck me
that our affair was over.

It's like that with physical work –
the neurons go firing off
on little routes of their own,
drawing their conclusions,
elbowing things up to the surface
with the force of magic.

That's why I phoned you that morning
and slipped you the black spot –
'Out of the blue,' you said,
'before we could say knife.'
Then I squared my shoulders,
and went back to my broom and shovel –

wondering: do I know my own mind?
Do they ever make mistakes,
those conjuring brainwaves?
I might have spoken aloud
for I was soon under scrutiny
from the knowing eyes of the fancy rats.

The Upper Hand

I am frightened of this orderly.
Huge, with a black helmet of hair,
she slaps her broom round my bed
and, fixing me with a glittering eye,
intones something gnomic.

'Sorry?' I keep saying, and at last
the words fall into focus:
'Two pints of lager
and a packet of crisps.'
I laugh obediently, mime sudden sleep.

Now she is here again, smacking my locker,
bending over me, her face
close as an eye surgeon's.
'Are you with me,' she breathes,
'or with the Woolwich?'

'With you,' I say fervently.

I Am Not Myself Today...

something has gone awry overnight –
some maladaptation of hormones, or a shift
in the mineral balance of the blood.

Scruples have invaded me
and something painful called tenderness.

I reach out to people I know;
but they wince away, wide-eyed.

How I repent yesterday's bitchiness,
its infidelities, its insobriety.

Look at my hand, steady as a rock
and holding out flowers;

but where has everyone gone?

At Madame Tussaud's

Seeing you in wax is a shock.
I hadn't realised you were here.

You stare glassily North-West,
with a slight curl of the lip.

The hand is excellently done, it reminds me
of certain intimacies, certain afternoons

in that room with the faulty light switch
and the purple sheets. We closed the blinds

and locked the doors. Love is so athletic –
a wine glass toppled in some amorous antic.

Afterwards there were drab days:
counsellors, consolers, a cold decline from your sun.

Here in wax you are all dignity and tailoring.
Thoughtfully I lean forward and start

to undress you, hardly noticing the faces
swivelling towards me. I work my way

through garment after garment, like a doctor
whose patient cannot help himself.

Elephants

Events loom towards you
blocking out the light like elephants –
births, deaths, weddings;
an appointment for root canal work.
A proposal. A diagnosis.

You've got to get past the date marked X
and then you're free until the next elephant
grows from a speck on the horizon
to a presence, towering between you
and the ordinary washing on the line.

Keeping on Top of Things

I want to be alone. But I have to see
the chiropodist, the dentist,
the car mechanic, the ear-syringer,
the roofer, the window cleaner,
and a man to cut back the creeper
which is forcing its way in
through the bedroom window.

Thank goodness I don't have to see
the manicurist, the otologist,
the arboriculturalist,
the reflexologist, the phrenologist
the hypnotherapist, the gynaecologist
the Chinese herbalist, or the psychiatrist –

at least not this week.

Next Please

Child power is overwhelming
the parents. Even the baby –
a prize marrow with a threatening eye –
is sucking the substance out of them;
and the toddlers are little Caligulas.

Grown-ups know their days
are numbered. Soon, with a dislocating yawn,
the children will swallow them,
leaving only shadows walking about
pretending to be sensible.

Wanting Gertie

Substantial in her white overall,
freckled as a trout,
Gertie bicycles through my dream
smelling of Mansion Polish and toast.

She pedals past me in her sturdy shoes
exuding goodness and good sense,
dwindling as I awake, calling her
to come back, come back.

Among the Dead Men

Wisps of mist are tenuous
round this solid boat-like shape
but the crashings are not waves.

We move intricately,
each feeding a dark orifice
from a hoarded, gleaming cache.

A man beside me, grey-moustached, limping,
wishes he too could be recycled:
'I'd drop myself in, no sweat.'

We are the reflective ones:
not for us the showy swing
of the ship-christener;

not for us the winners'
hubristic champagne-showers,
the profligate, heady waste.

We know about quiet change
and renewal. Or at least
we are making a gesture towards it.

Mésalliance

I am divorcing my dog.
He never cared for me: we were
unsuited. His lickspittle allegiance
lies wetly elsewhere, his easy bonhomie
bounces over others.

I am barely acknowledged:
a mere opener of tins,
prison warder, valet.
In front of other dogs
he is insubordinate.

I mean to dispose of him
by auction. He suspects this:
snuffs and sighs as I batten down
for the evening. (A window left ajar
and he's gone.)

The back-up plan involves garden work.
He peers into my excavations
glaucous-eyed and curious,
but feints and weaves at my attempts
to catch and measure him.

Carer

He's so old now. I suppose
he must be mine. I can't remember

giving birth, but his face
stares up from dusty photographs.

He spoons my soup, tucks my
blankets round me at night.

Of course I cannot leave the house.
The hedges are full of creeping things,

park railings line up against me;
the neighbours itch to snatch my key.

My son, my single link to life.
If I killed him, he could be free.

Good Girl

She sleeps in the box room
in Mrs Johnson's house. She is twelve years old
but growing younger every day
away from home. Letters from her mother
are pale and creased with wear:
(*Be very good and when we get some petrol
we'll come and see you. Tigger sends his love.*)

Mr Rainey, the lodger, gives her a yellow smile
over the breakfast toast, while the others
rush off to their war-work.
Plump-fingered, silver-haired,
with something dark staining his waistcoat,
he divides his butter ration
into seven greasy morsels.

One morning she wakes to panic – a pool of blood
on the sheets, a fierce, gripping ache,
a hot wave of fear and shame.
She shuts herself in until Mrs J. comes home
and reassures her. *It's just growing up dear.*
Mysterious accessories, elaborate with elastic.
The sheets taken away with a tired sigh.

The bathroom is down a dim, narrow passage, a place
of awkward passings and pleasantries.
Coming out one day carrying something
shaming and private behind her back,
she comes face to face with Mr Rainey,
who puts a doughy hand on her shoulder.
I know what you'd like my dear. Ginger biscuits.

You must come and have tea in my room.
She runs to the kitchen stove, that temperamental
comforter and incinerator. She knows
she must accept: that is what
is meant by being good. So at four o'clock
he leans over her with his plate of biscuits.
His sardine breath shuts off the air.

Reunion

Walking round Kew with your mother
was tough. Why did you bring her?
Wasn't it difficult enough,
our meeting after twenty years apart?

Of course it was kind of her to point things out,
the statuary, the oriental wildfowl, the ice house,
the way the children were running about,
the way the weather was getting worse.

Lacunae? Not with your mother to take
advantage of each pause. Our swallowed words
lay heavy as rocks. Silence flew off
over the lake like a flock of birds.

Friend

(i.m. Margaret Budleigh)

Our friendship lasted more than forty years:
it wound between us like a golden thread
which never broke or loosened. You'll live on
in gestures we remember, times we shared.
Larkin was right: however we may grieve,
we know that what survives of us is love.

Musical Chairs

Whirling round we go,
though some of us don't like
the music. Some of us
don't even like the game, but
one by one we are spun off
into the dusk, where the laughter
echoes more faintly, the distant
fluted melodies modulate
to a minor key, the red balloons
and the yellow balloons
are losing their lustre
and the air thins out across the grass
to where the cliff shelves down
suddenly, the samphire clinging
to the crumbling edge. The sea below
is advancing and receding. It has
its own game, which is called
swallowing and scavenging.

Convalescence

Nothing could make her love him.
To cure himself of the pain
he hired a man (thin, hungry, voluble)
to speak ill of her from dawn to dusk.

Once a week the man stayed all night,
murmuring aspersions, sleeping in snatches
on a rattan chair. No change.
The man left, the obsession did not.

But one Tuesday, he awoke refreshed.
What was his beloved's name? It had slipped
his mind. He stood at the window, marvelling
at the oleander buds unfolding towards the sun.